BUILDING CARDBOARD DOLLHOUSES

Other books by the same author

DESIGNING HOUSES
Les Walker and Jeff Milstein
The Overlook Press
Woodstock, New York
12498

A handbook for the layman on the design of personal dwelling

BUILDING CARDBOARD DOLLHOUSES

Written, photographed and illustrated by

Jeff Milstein

HARPER COLOPHON BOOKS

Harper & Row, Publishers
New York, Hagerstown, San Francisco, London

BUILDING CARDBOARD DOLLHOUSES. Copyright © 1978 by Jeffrey Milstein. All rights reserved. Printed in the United States of America. No part of this book may be used or reproduced in any manner without written permission except in the case of brief quotations embodied in critical articles and reviews. For information address Harper & Row, Publishers, Inc., 10 East 53rd Street, New York, N.Y. 10022. Published simultaneously in Canada by Fitzhenry & Whiteside Limited, Toronto.

First HARPER COLOPHON edition published 1978

LIBRARY OF CONGRESS CATALOG NUMBER: 78-19235
ISBN: 0-06-090612-X

78 79 80 81 82 10 9 8 7 6 5 4 3 2 1

Contents

6 INTRODUCTION

8 GATHERING SUPPLIES
10 Corrugated Cardboard
11 Poster Board
12 Tools & Materials

14 BUILDING YOUR DOLLHOUSE
16 Laying out the Plans
17 Making a Pattern
18 Cutting out the Pieces
22 Scoring & Folding
24 Painting
26 Assembling the Pieces

32 PLANS FOR 5 HOUSES
33 Notes on the Plans
34 Colonial Dollhouse
42 Georgian Dollhouse
50 Greek Revival Dollhouse
58 Victorian Dollhouse
70 Italianate Dollhouse

79 APPENDIX

Introduction

Ever since I can remember I built things out of cardboard, paper, and glue. My first cardboard toy was a garage my father made for me to keep my toy cars in. I was about five then. Now I'm grown up and I'm still making cardboard models and toys. I became an architect and improved my cardboard building techniques along the way, and in this book I want to show you how you can create your own handsome and surprisingly sturdy dollhouses out of free or inexpensive cardboard. All the dollhouses in this book were made from corrugated cardboard and poster board. By following the step-by-step directions you will learn how to cut out, glue, paint, and assemble your own dollhouse at a fraction of the cost of a store-bought one. You don't need any special skills or expensive tools and you can make them in your own living room with the whole family taking part. Though the finished house is fun to look at and play with, you may find the most fun of all is the building and decorating process itself.

But that's not all. The book is also a mini-history lesson on American architectural styles. Each house is designed to represent one of the major styles of houses popular between 1700 and 1900. Beginning with colonial, the styles include Georgian, Greek Revival, Victorian, and Italianate. A brief historical description is included with the plans of each house

Chapter 1
GATHERING SUPPLIES

One of the major advantages of building cardboard dollhouses is that you don't need much in the way of tools and materials. Here is what you will need, and where to find it.

Corrugated Cardboard

Corrugated cardboard is the basic building material for the houses. It is used for walls, floors, roofs, porches, chimneys, and even window and door frames. In its most common form corrugated cardboard is made up of 3 pieces of paper: the middle piece, which is corrugated, is glued at the ridges to the top and bottom papers. The corrugated center acts like the web of a truss or beam, giving the cardboard its strength. Although corrugated cardboard is relatively strong, it must be handled with some care to prevent bending or crushing.

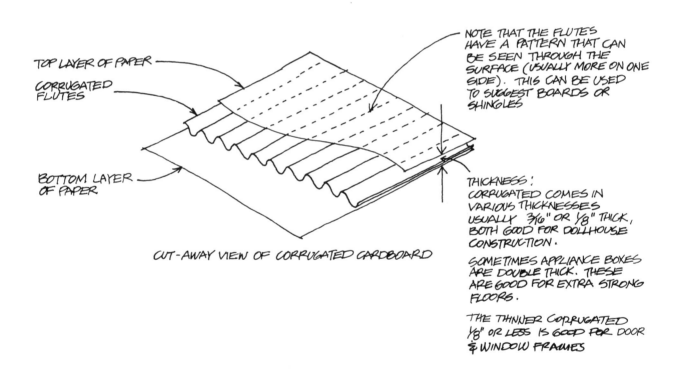

Where to find:
If you can scavenge a bit you can get it free. Supermarkets, drugstores, liquor and hardware stores are good bets. Store managers are usually delighted to get empty cartons off their hands. Appliance and furniture stores are good for big pieces. If you want brand new big flat pieces you can try an art supply store or order by mail from Charrette (see Appendix). All the houses in the book were made from a $14.50-package mailed from Charrette.

Poster Board

This is a lightweight, inexpensive, common cardboard like the board that comes back with laundered shirts. It is not as strong as corrugated but it is good for details, such as door and window frames and decoration. It comes in several different thicknesses. The thicker boards show more shadow detail but the thinner boards are easier to cut, especially for curves. Get some light and medium weight.

Where to find:
Laundered shirts, gift boxes, or purchased at art supply, stationery, or five-and-ten-cent stores.

Tools & Materials

Here are the basic tools and materials you will need. Most things you probably already have lying around somewhere. Anything else you need you can probably find at your local art supply or stationery store.

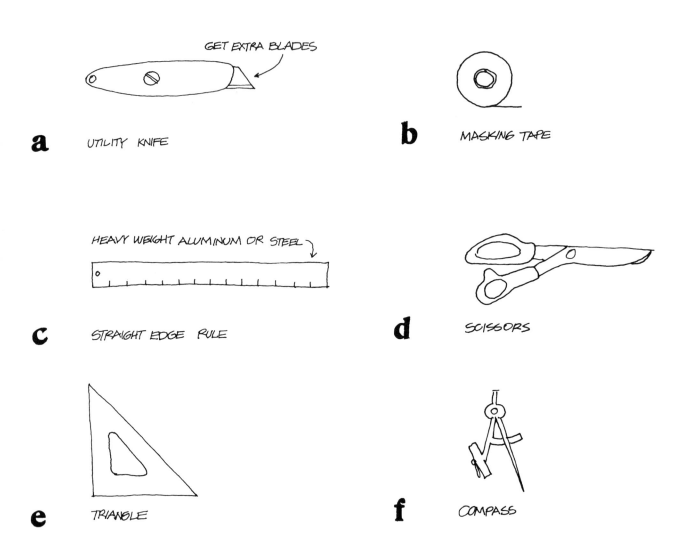

a UTILITY KNIFE

b MASKING TAPE

c STRAIGHT EDGE RULE

d SCISSORS

e TRIANGLE

f COMPASS

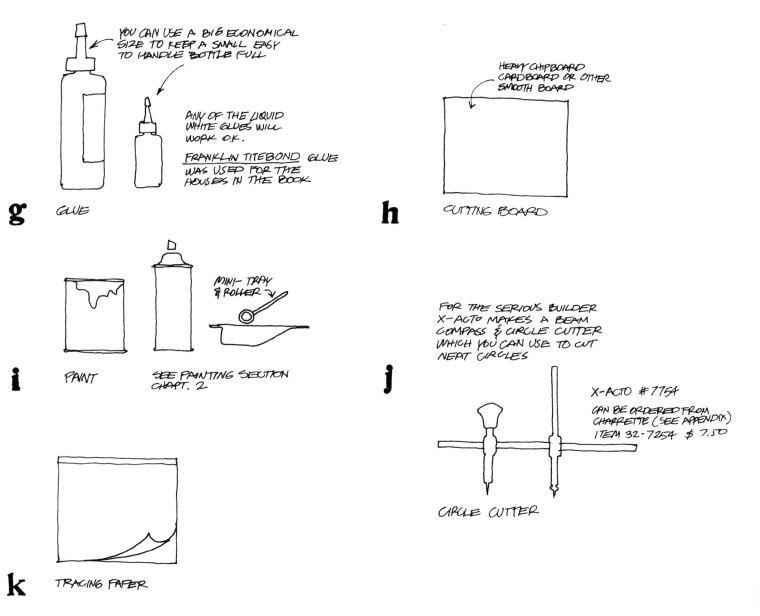

Chapter 2
BUILDING YOUR DOLLHOUSE

This chapter describes the basic steps for building a cardboard dollhouse using plans from the book or a design of your own. Find a comfortable, well-lit place to work. A big table is helpful, or you can work on the floor.

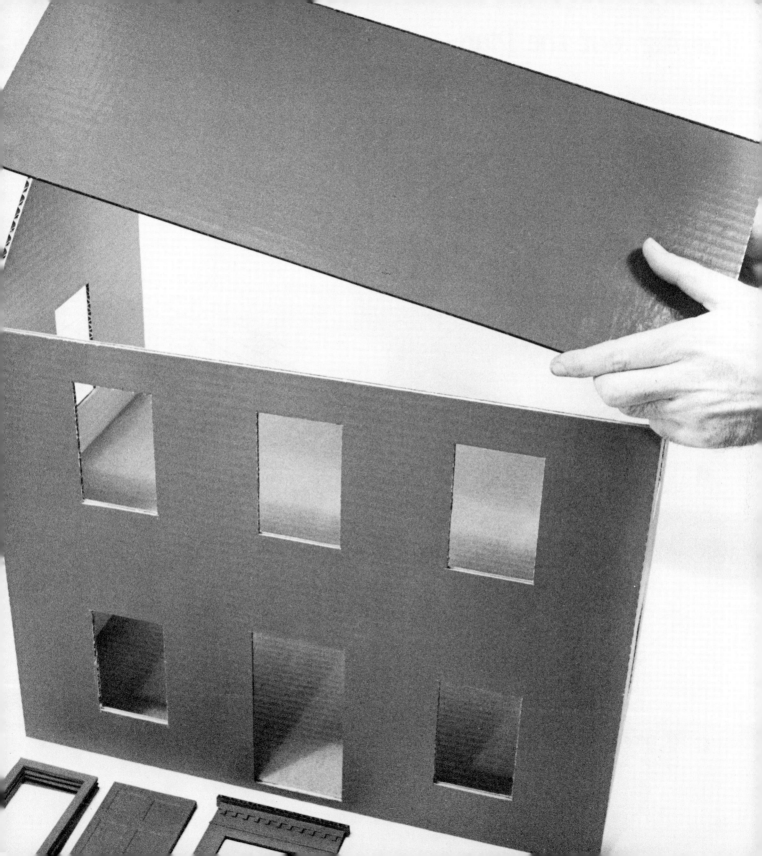

Laying out the Plans

The first step is to draw the plans on the cardboard so the parts can be cut out. Use a sharp pencil and draw lightly first. The example shown is the laying-out of an arched door and windows for the front wall of a dollhouse. First cut a rectangular piece the size of the wall. Use your triangle to be sure that the corners are square. If you have a T-square it will save you some time. Otherwise, follow the steps below for laying out without a T-square.

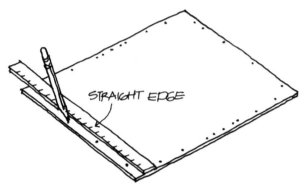

a MAKE MARKS ALONG EDGES OF CARDBOARD LOCATING VERTICAL & HORIZONTAL DIMENSIONS FOR WINDOWS & DOORS

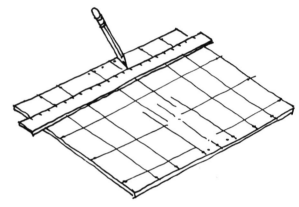

b CONNECT THE OPPOSITE POINTS WITH THE STRAIGHT EDGE AND DRAW LIGHT LINES ACROSS THE BOARD LOCATING THE OUTLINES OF WINDOWS & DOORS.

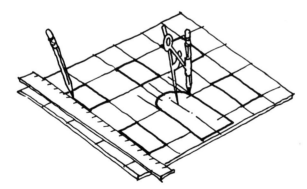

c GO BACK AND DARKEN THE SHAPES TO BE CUT OUT. USE A COMPASS TO DRAW CURVED SHAPES

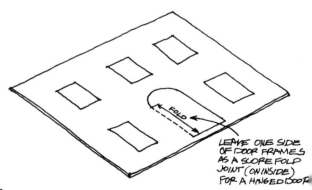

d NOW YOU ARE READY TO CUT OUT THE DOOR & WINDOWS.

LEAVE ONE SIDE OF DOOR FRAMES AS A SCORE FOLD JOINT (ON INSIDE) FOR A HINGED DOOR

Making a Pattern

Decorative pieces can easily be drawn up with this tracing paper method. The important thing to remember is that it is not necessary that decorative patterns be exact copies of the book plans. Shown below is an example of how you would draw a piece of gingerbread decoration. Try making your own.

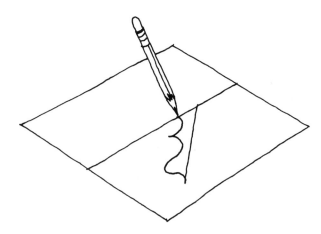

a DRAW HALF OF THE PATTERN ON A PIECE OF TRACING PAPER

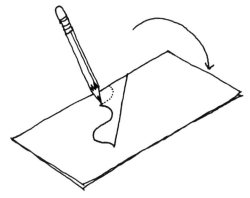

b FOLD THE TRACING PAPER ON THE LINE & TRACE THE IMAGE

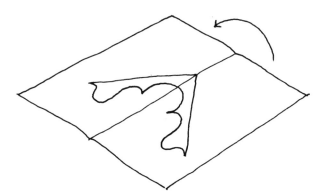

c UNFOLD THE PAPER & YOU HAVE A SYMMETRICAL IMAGE. USE CARBON PAPER OR A SOFT PENCIL ON THE BACK TO TRANSFER THE IMAGE.

Cutting out the Pieces

Here are some pointers that will help you to cut out the pieces you have drawn up. Place the cardboard to be cut on a piece of heavy chipboard or smooth plywood cutting board. If the cutting board surface is rough, you will find that the bottom of the cardboard tears as the cut is made. Tearing is also a sign that the blade is dull. Draw the blade across the surface the first time pressing moderately, cutting the top surface. Then repeat the cut. The blade will want to stay in the slot you made on the first cut. 2 or 3 draws, depending on the blade condition, will cut the piece.

Cutting out curved shapes is not too difficult if you just go slowly along the line, making several passes for each cut, without trying to cut too deeply at once. On thin cardboard you can use a pair of scissors.

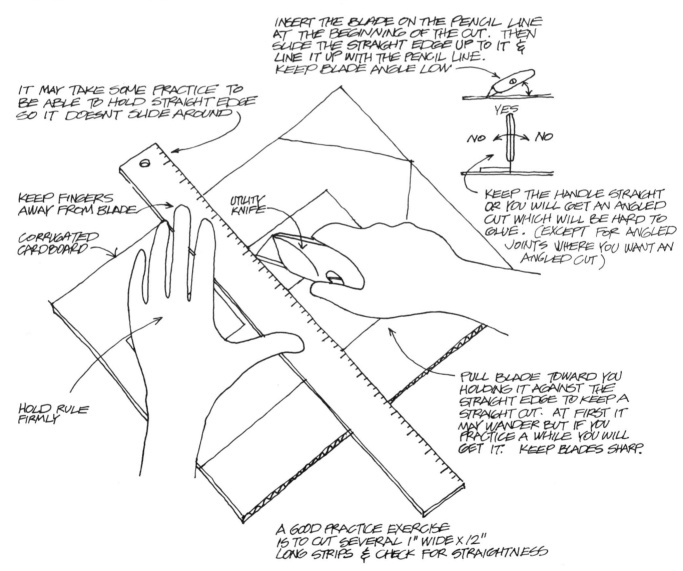

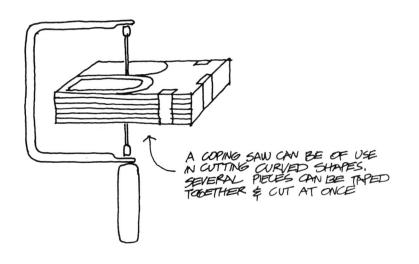

A COPING SAW CAN BE OF USE IN CUTTING CURVED SHAPES. SEVERAL PIECES CAN BE TAPED TOGETHER & CUT AT ONCE

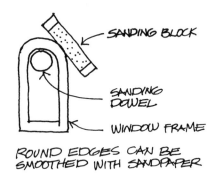

ROUND EDGES CAN BE SMOOTHED WITH SANDPAPER

WHEN CUTTING OUT A SERIES OF WINDOW FRAMES LAY OUT IN ROWS AS BELOW. CUT OUT THE CENTERS FIRST THEN SEPARATE FRAMES

WHEN CUTTING OUT CENTERS START AT ONE CORNER THEN PULL BACK FROM OPPOSITE CORNER. TURN OVER & NICK THE CORNERS TO EASE REMOVAL OF CENTER PIECE.

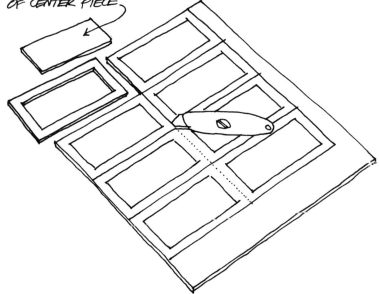

WHEN FITTING ANGLED JOINTS, A BETTER JOINT IS MADE BY CUTTING ONE OF THE PIECES AT AN ANGLE AS SHOWN.

AN ALTERNATE TECHNIQUE IS TO FLATTEN THE EDGE WHERE CONTACT IS MADE BY PULLING A HARD BLUNT OBJECT ACROSS THE EDGE

PULL ACROSS EDGE CRUSHING THE CORNER

Scoring & Folding

Although the plans show walls and floors as separate pieces, whenever you have a big enough piece of cardboard, you can score and fold the wall and floor joints. This is easier and neater than gluing. Chimneys, roof peaks, and porches should be made with folds whenever possible.

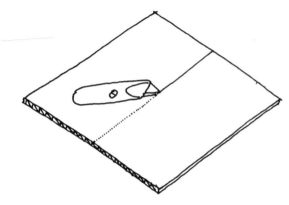

a CUT THROUGH TOP SIDE & CORRUGATIONS BUT BE CAREFUL NOT TO CUT THROUGH BOTTOM PAPER. PRACTICE A FEW.

b PULL THE ROUND END OF A PENCIL ACROSS THE CUT SEVERAL TIMES CRUSHING THE CORRUGATIONS.

NOW YOU CAN FOLD THE CARDBOARD MAKING A NEAT CORNER.

FOR EXTRA STRENGTH PUT GLUE IN THE JOINT.

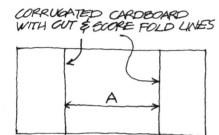

ONE POINT TO NOTE IS THAT AFTER FOLDED, THE INSIDE DIMENSION SHRINKS & THE OUTSIDE GETS WIDER BY AN AMOUNT EQUAL TO THE THICKNESS OF THE CORRUGATED.

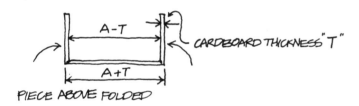

PIECE ABOVE FOLDED

Painting

The key to a good paint job is the undercoat. You must prime corrugated cardboard with an alcohol base, quick-drying primer (see below). This is absolutely necessary; otherwise the cardboard will absorb the paint and give a poor finish. It is much easier to paint the parts before they are assembled. A small roller is an excellent way to apply primer and paint. Spray paint is good, especially for small pieces. But if you spray, be sure to do it outside, where you can avoid inhaling the vapors. Once the surface is primed, you can use either oil or latex paint. Oil will give a brighter finish but latex is less messy and has no odor. You can make you own wallpaper by drawing right on the painted surface with felt-tip pens or you can glue on wallpaper made from wrapping paper, printed fabric, scraps of real wallpaper, or adhesive backed shelf paper.

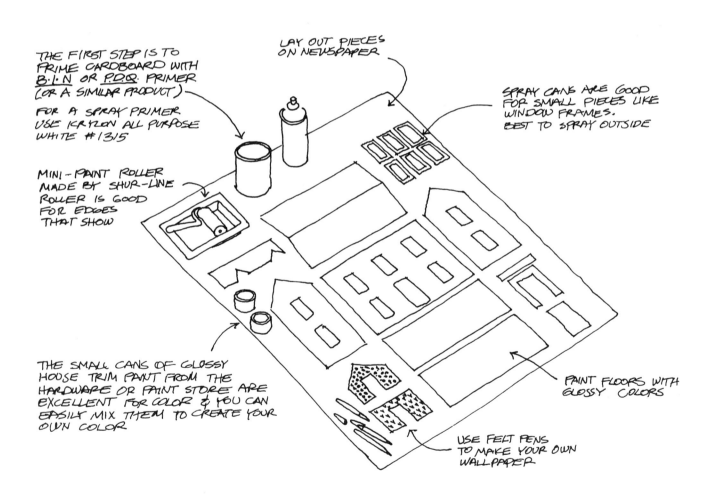

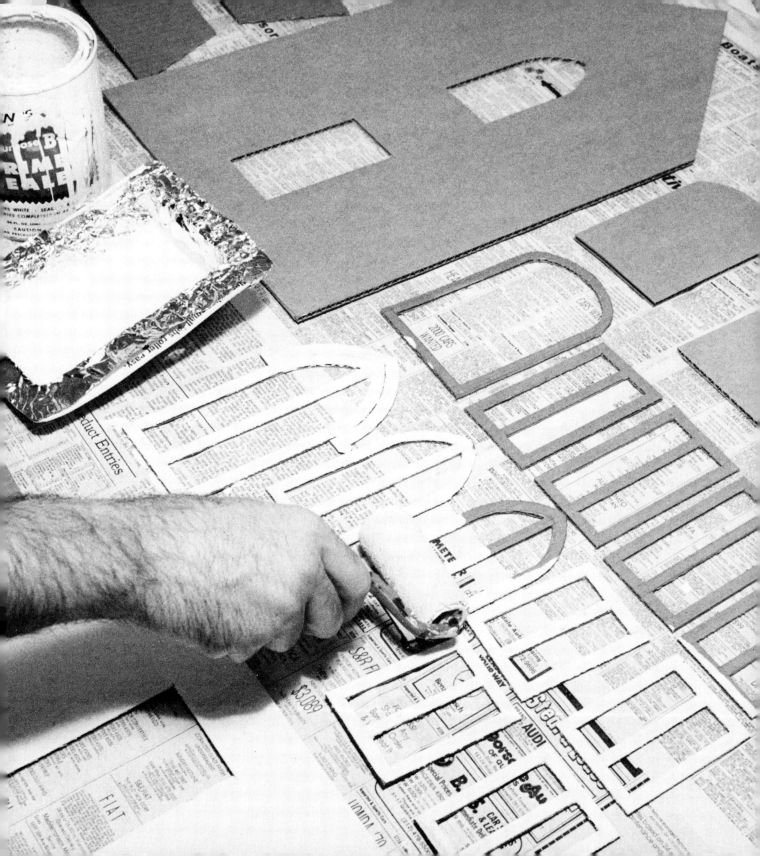

Assembling the Pieces

After you have painted all the pieces and drawn or glued wallpaper to the inside (if desired) you are ready to assemble. The assembly steps for a simple dollhouse are shown below. The same principles can be applied to more complex dollhouses. Keep a damp rag handy to wipe glue off fingers and cardboard.

BEFORE GLUING THE PIECES CHECK THAT THE EDGES ARE STRAIGHT & SQUARE. IF THE CUTS ARE ANGLED AS SHOWN HERE THEY WON'T MAKE GOOD CONTACT FOR GLUING

USE A PIECE OF SANDPAPER WRAPPED AROUND A WOOD BLOCK TO SQUARE UP BAD CUTS THAT WILL BE GLUE JOINTS.

SANDING BLOCK

APPLYING GLUE:

APPLY GLUE TO BOTH PIECES TO BE GLUED. SQUEEZE THE BOTTLE WHILE PULLING IT ALONG THE EDGE. RUN YOUR FINGER LIGHTLY OVER THE BEAD TO SPREAD IT OUT. ON THE FLAT SIDE.

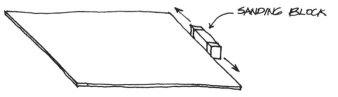

GLUE BEAD

FINGER

ON THE NARROW EDGE RUB THE NOZZLE BACK & FORTH TO APPLY THE GLUE. TAP FINGER ALONG THE EDGE TO SPREAD OUT

a THE FIRST STEP IS TO GLUE THE WINDOW & DOOR FRAMES TO THE WALLS AND THE 2ND FLOOR SUPPORTS TO THE INSIDE OF THE WALLS
(YOU CAN ALSO WAIT UNTILL THE HOUSE IS ASSEMBLED TO ADD THE TRIM FRAMES.)

b GLUE FRONT WALL TO FLOOR

ATTACH PIECES OF MASKING TAPE (BEFORE GLUING) TO BOTTOM OF FLOOR. PULL THEM UP AND AROUND TO HOLD WALL TIGHT WHILE DRYING.

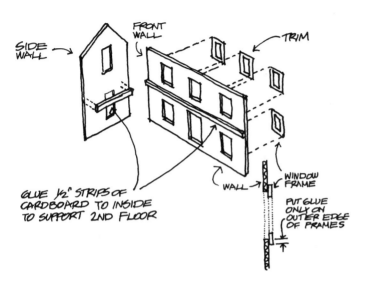
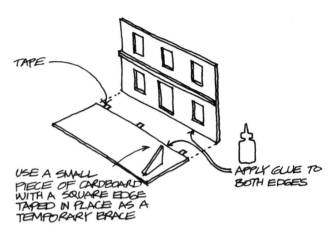

c NEXT ADD A SIDE WALL. USE TAPE AS ABOVE TO HOLD WHILE DRYING

d NOW ADD THE THIRD WALL. REMOVE TAPE AFTER 10 MIN. BE CAREFUL NOT TO TEAR CARDBOARD

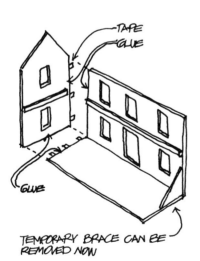
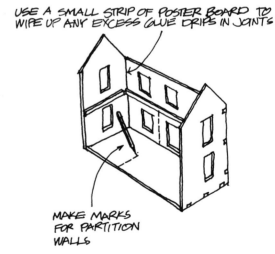

e ADD FIRST FLOOR WALL PARTITIONS AND THEN ADD SECOND FLOOR

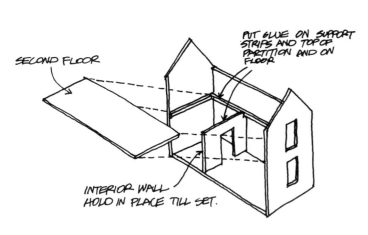

f ADD SECOND FLOOR PARTITIONS AND ROOF. USE TAPE TO HOLD ROOF DOWN WHILE DRYING

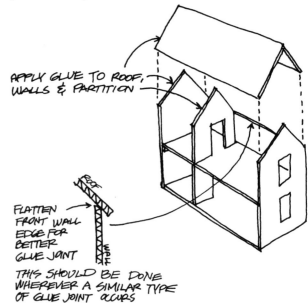

g ADD CHIMNEYS, DECORATION, PORCHES, ETC.

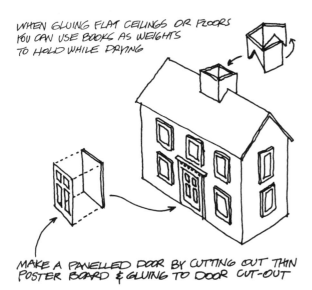

Chapter 3
PLANS for 5 DOLLHOUSES

This chapter contains dollhouse plans and a brief historical description for five classic American houses. These designs were chosen because they represent the major trends in the development of American residential architecture from Colonial times to 1900.

In designing the dollhouses, it was the intention to capture the essence of the style rather than to keep the dimensions historically exact. In order to make a usable dollhouse that can accommodate standard furniture, interior partitions that would make the rooms too small are left out. The interior decoration is left to the builder's imagination. See the appendix for mail order houses that sell interior furnishings.

The dollhouse colors shown on the cover of the book represent traditional colors. You can use these, but you should feel free to use more decorative colors if you like.

Notes for the Plans

The plans plans are drawn at a scale of 1/8" = 1", except for door and window frames, and some details which are drawn at ¼" = 1". Some parts are shown as full size patterns.

The numbers are dimensions in inches.

The cardboard to be used is corrugated except where noted.

Although floors are shown in the plans as single thickness, they can be made double thick for extra strength by gluing two pieces together.

The dimensions are based on corrugated cardboard 3/16" thick. If thicker or thinner board is used certain dimensions may have to be adjusted slightly.

Where the direction of the corrugated flutes is important to the design, the symbol of the flutes is shown by the symbol: ≡

A score/fold line (see Chapt. 2) is shown by: ─ FOLD ─

The center line of a symmetrical part is shown by: ₵

For some pieces the cut should be angled to make a neater joint. The angled cuts are shown by:

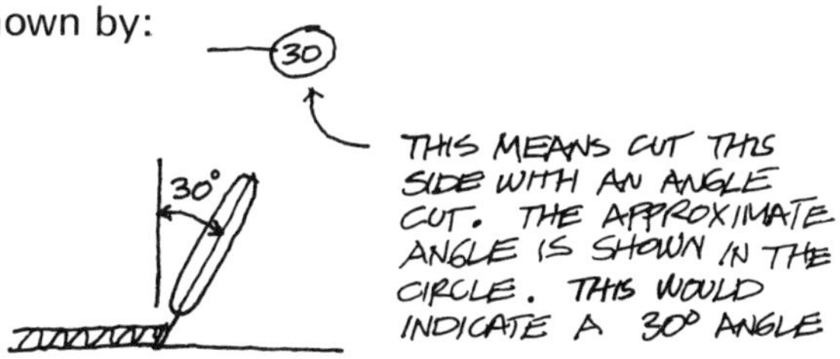

THIS MEANS CUT THIS SIDE WITH AN ANGLE CUT. THE APPROXIMATE ANGLE IS SHOWN IN THE CIRCLE. THIS WOULD INDICATE A 30° ANGLE

1 Colonial

There were many types of colonial houses built beginning with the seventeenth century. The most popular style in New England was the simple frame house with a large central chimney, two rooms upstairs, and two rooms downstairs. The houses were sturdily constructed to last a long time. Built on a foundation of fieldstone and brick, they were framed with heavy oak timbers. The walls were covered with clapboards or shingles. The interior walls were covered with board or plaster. The plans were symmetrical with the entry door in the center. The early houses were functional and devoid of decoration. Later, decoration was added in the form of interior paneling, hand-turned stair balusters and newel posts. Outside decoration was mostly around the entry door in the form of decorated door pediments. In later years, the colonists added lean-tos to the back for more space, creating the salt-box shape.

This dollhouse is the easiest of five to build. It is representative of a style popular around the first part of the 18th century, that had some front door decoration. Colonial houses were generally left unpainted or painted a deep red-iron oxide color.

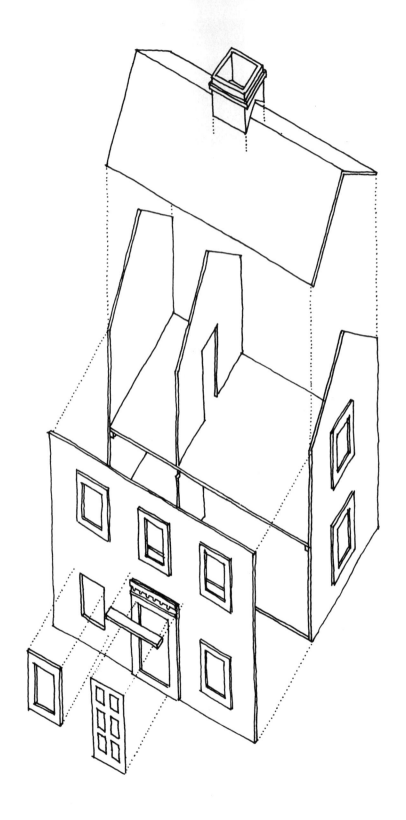

Assembly

1. Glue 2nd floor support strips to inside of walls.

2. Glue walls & first floor together.

3. Add first floor interior partition and 2nd floor.

4. Add 2nd floor interior partition.

5. Glue on roof. Be sure it is centered and side walls are vertical.

6. Assemble chimney, add drip course, and glue to center of roof.

7. Glue door panel cut-out to door. Glue door frame assembly together and add to front wall.

8. Add window frames.

Plans

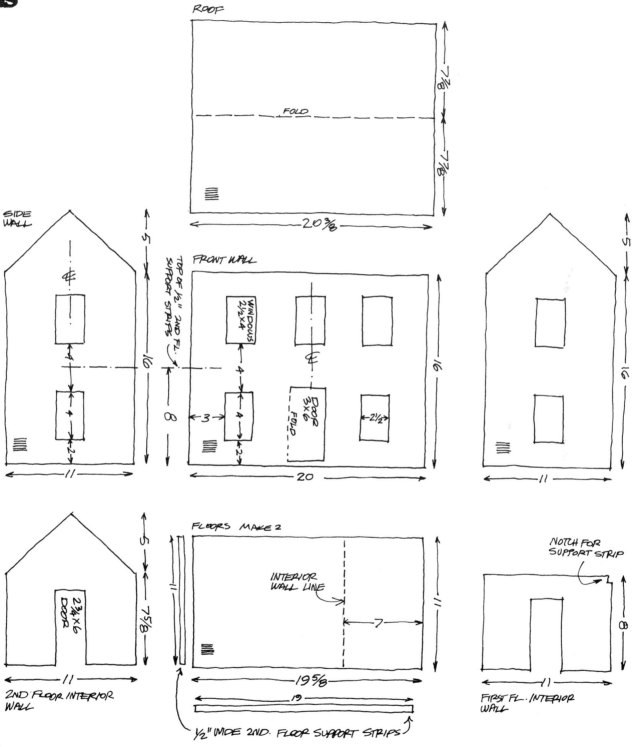

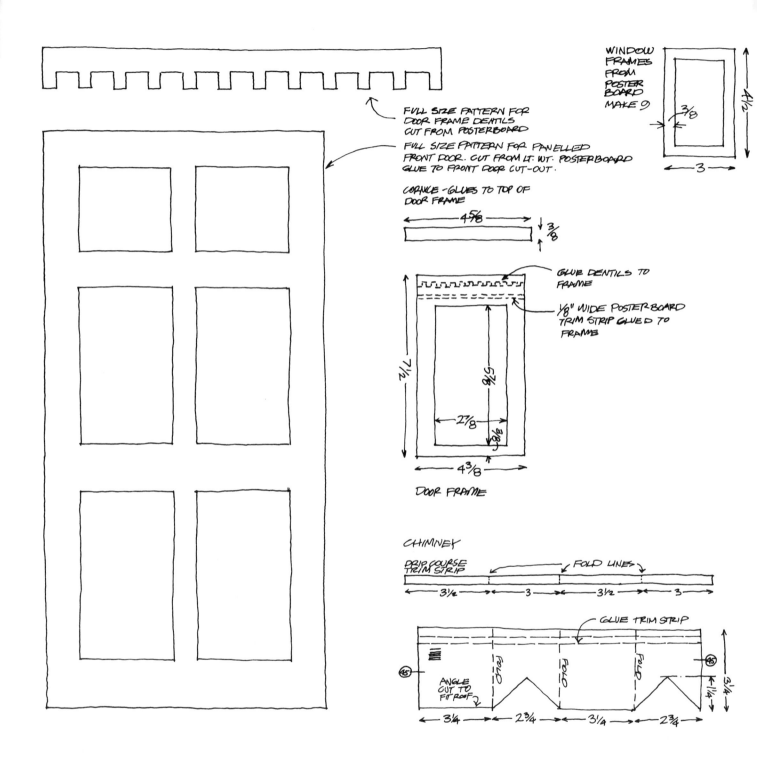

2 Georgian

In the 1720s a more ornate style, named for the first four Georges of England, became popular as a result of the introduction to Americans of handbooks on house carpentry and architecture.

The typical Georgian house was symmetrical with a hipped or gable roof. The major difference between the plan of the colonial and the Georgian was the Georgian central hall, made possible by removing the central chimney and locating a chimney in each end wall. The front entrances were ornately decorated with pediments and semi-circular windows called fan lights. The central second floor window was often a curved window, called a "Palladian" window. Columns or piers were often placed at the corners and on the sides of the front door. Small, evenly spaced blocks, called dentils, decorated the roof eaves. Georgian houses were constructed out of both wood and masonry. The wood houses were usually colored white or light pastels. The masonry houses were left natural. Some of the later Georgian houses were very lavishly decorated. With the American revolution, the Georgian style was simplified and became the federal style.

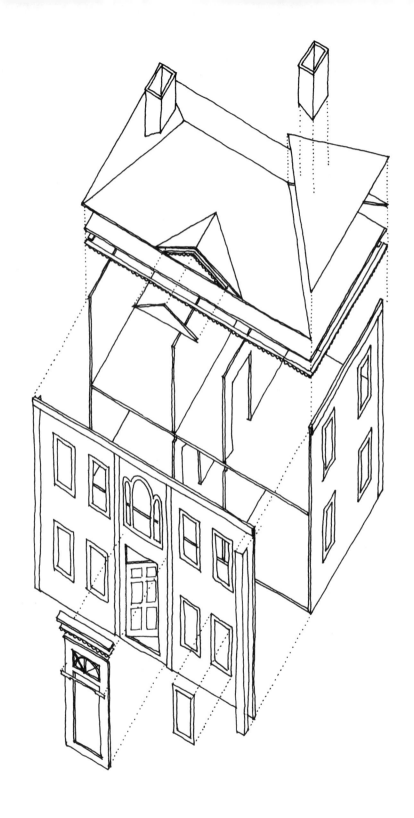

Assembly

1. Glue window frames to walls.

2. Glue poster board horizontal strips and vertical pilasters to walls. (The corner pilaster can be one piece with a score/fold.)

3. Glue 2nd floor support strips to inside of walls.

4. Glue exterior walls and first floor together.

5. Glue first floor interior partitions in place and add 2nd floor.

6. Glue 2nd floor interior partitions in place.

7. Glue ¼" dentil strips to 2nd floor ceiling. This makes a lip which fits over the walls. Glue ceiling into place on walls.

8. Assemble roof and glue to 2nd floor ceiling.

9. Add roof porticoe assembly over palladian window and add chimneys as shown.

10. Glue door panel cut-out to front door.

11. Assemble door frame transom window and pediment assembly. Glue to front wall.

Plans

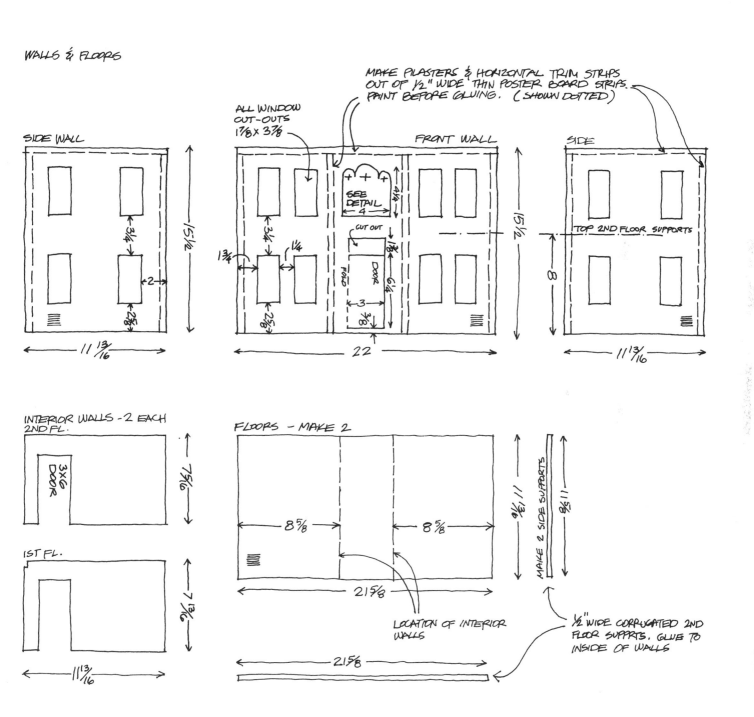

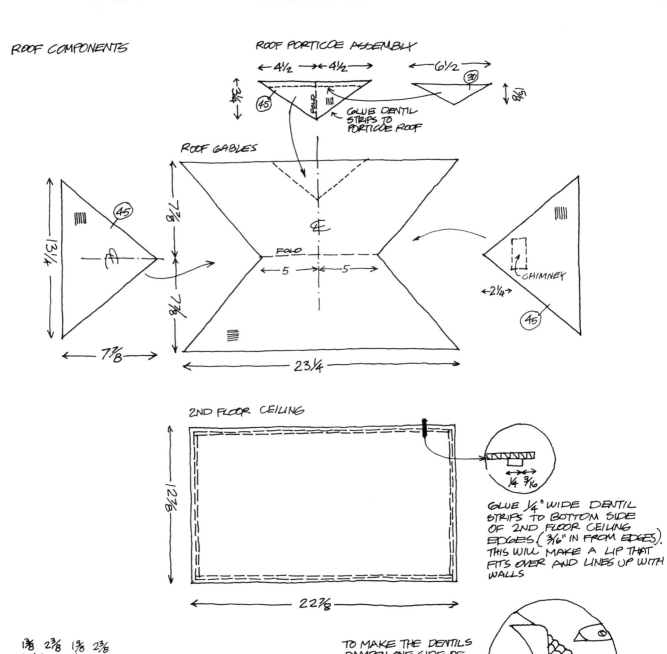

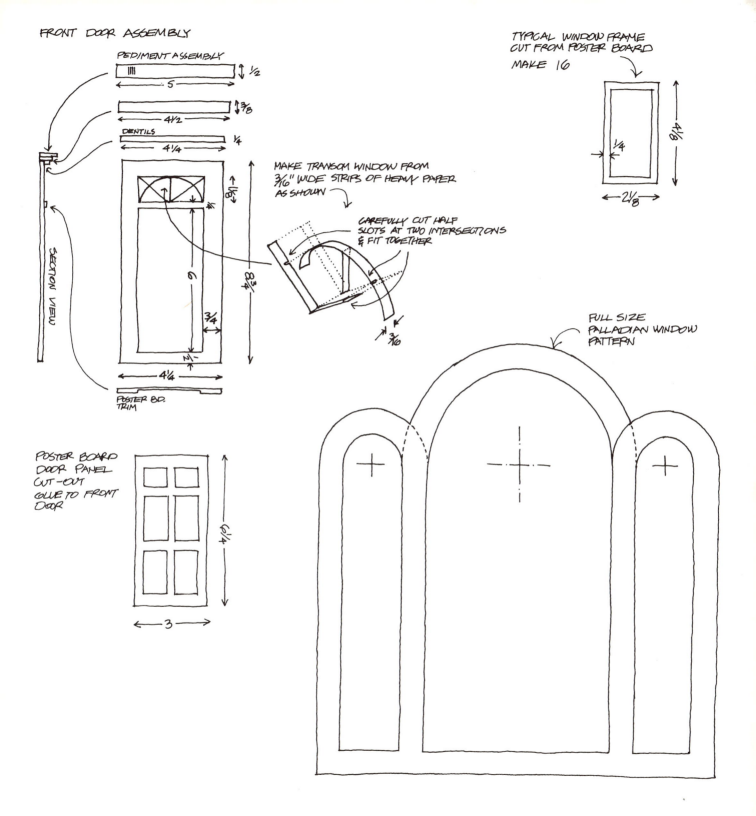

3 Greek Revival

Between 1820 and 1840 the American Greek Revival house became very popular. The idea was to make a house that resembled a Greek temple, since the Greek forms were thought to embody purity and the ideals of democracy. The architectural emphasis moved to the gabled end, where a large triangular pediment was supported by doric or ionic columns or pilasters all following classic Greek orders. Simpler and cleaner than Georgian, they were usually painted pure white. Most Greek Revival houses were wood frame with clapboards on the exterior. Many colonial style houses had Greek pediments added to their porches to make them conform to the popular style of the period.

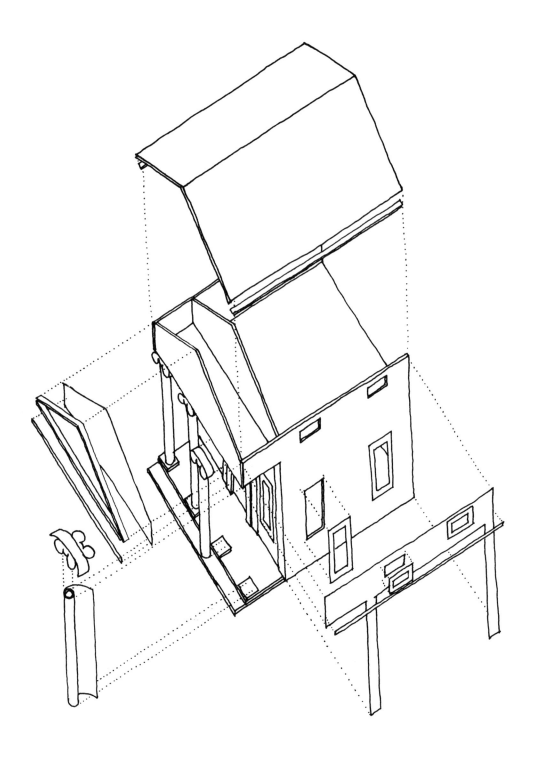

Assembly

1. Glue poster board trim and window and door trim to walls.

2. Glue 2nd floor support strips to inside of walls.

3. Assemble first floor, front wall and side walls. Add 2nd floor.

4. Glue porch pediment wall, with poster board cover, to side walls. Add porch ceiling.

5. Glue on roof so that it is even with wall at back and overhangs ½" at front. Glue side cornice strips to roof and walls.

6. Add corrugated cornice strips to pediment wall. Add 1/8" poster board trim strip to pediment and side walls.

7. Glue porch floor to first floor and glue column bases to porch floor.

8. Assemble columns as shown and glue into position between column base and porch ceiling. Use 1 1/8" x 1 1/8" poster board shims or trim column as required to get a snug fit.

Plans

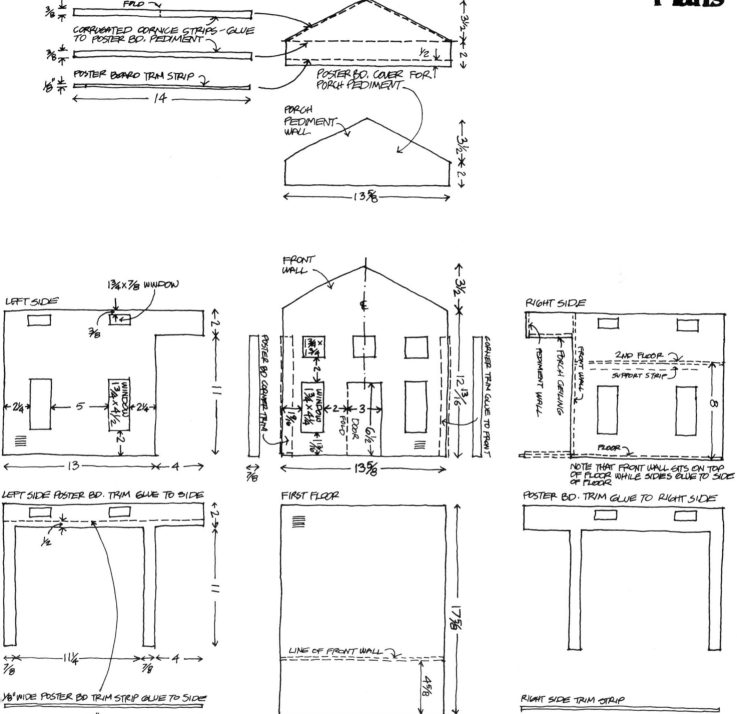

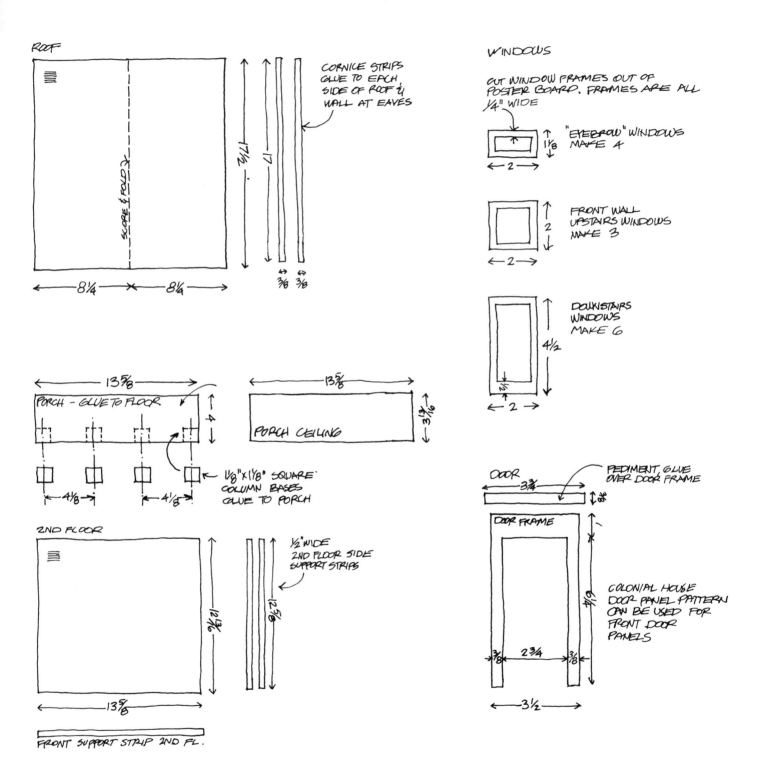

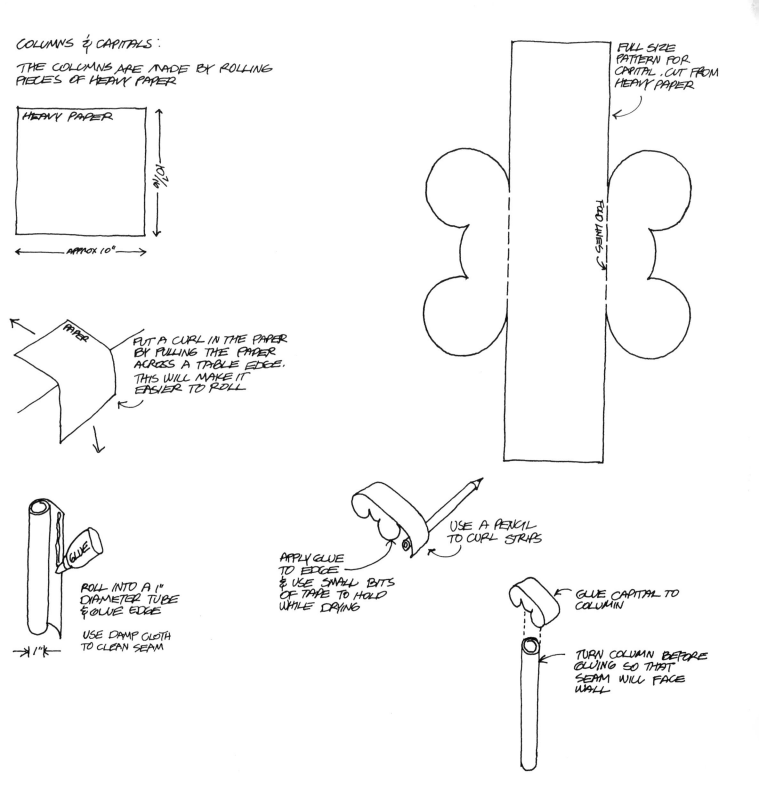

4 Victorian

Around 1830 the Greek Revival style began to give way to a variety of Victorian styles. All characterized by flamboyance and decoration, they were based on Tudor, Roman, Italian, French, and Old English styles.

The balloon frame, made of two by four's, became popular and carpenters got into sawn wood ornamentation known as gingerbread. These gingerbread designs depended more on the carpenter-builder's whim than on a rigid architectural style, and thus became known as carpenter gothic. The exteriors were finished in horizontal or vertical boards, sometimes with shingles. They were painted in a great variety of colors and shades. The Victorian dollhouse is an example of this popular style. This period culminated in the late 1890s with the most ornate, decorated, and spacious Victorian houses.

Assembly

1. Glue door battens, door frame and window frames to walls.

2. Glue 2nd floor support strips to inside of walls.

3. Glue walls and first floor together.

4. Add first floor interior partition and 2nd floor.

5. Add 2nd floor interior partition.

6. Glue on roof. Check to see that it is centered and side walls stay vertical.

7. Glue front gable to roof as shown.

8. Glue gingerbread roof trim into notch space on front and sides. Use bits of tape underneath to hold in place while drying.

9. Fold porch frame and glue to porch floor.

10. Glue porch frame and floor to wall.

11. Glue porch gingerbread trim to porch frame.

12. Glue porch gable to porch frame and front wall. Check from side to see that it is level at ridge. Add rest of porch roof as shown.

Plans

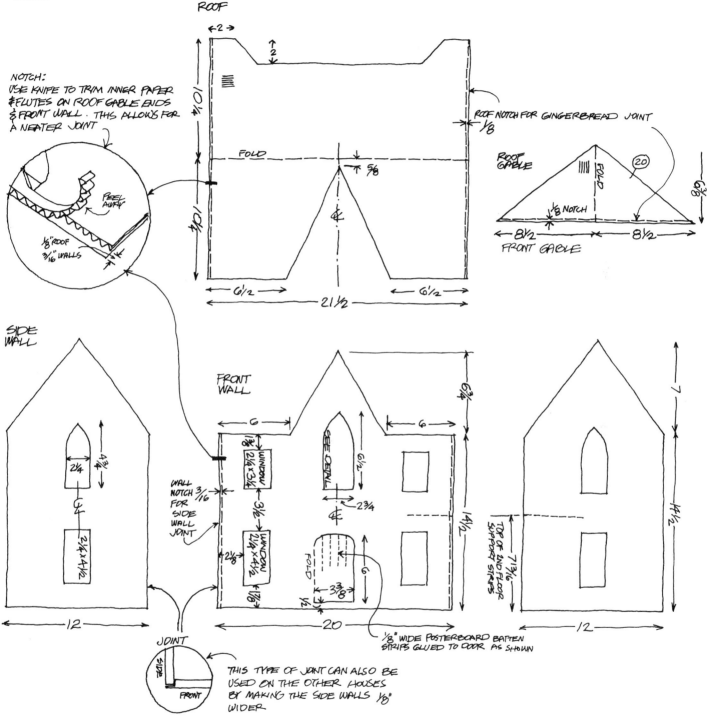

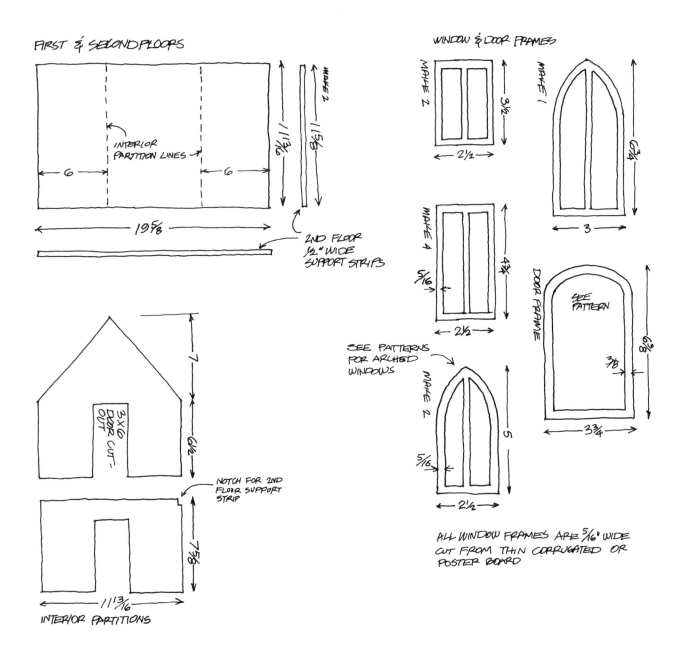

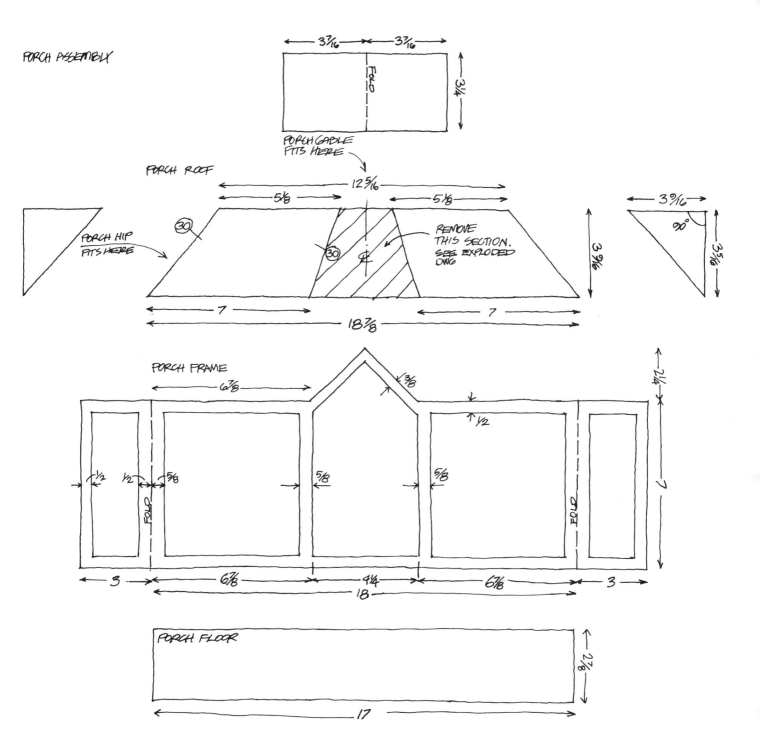

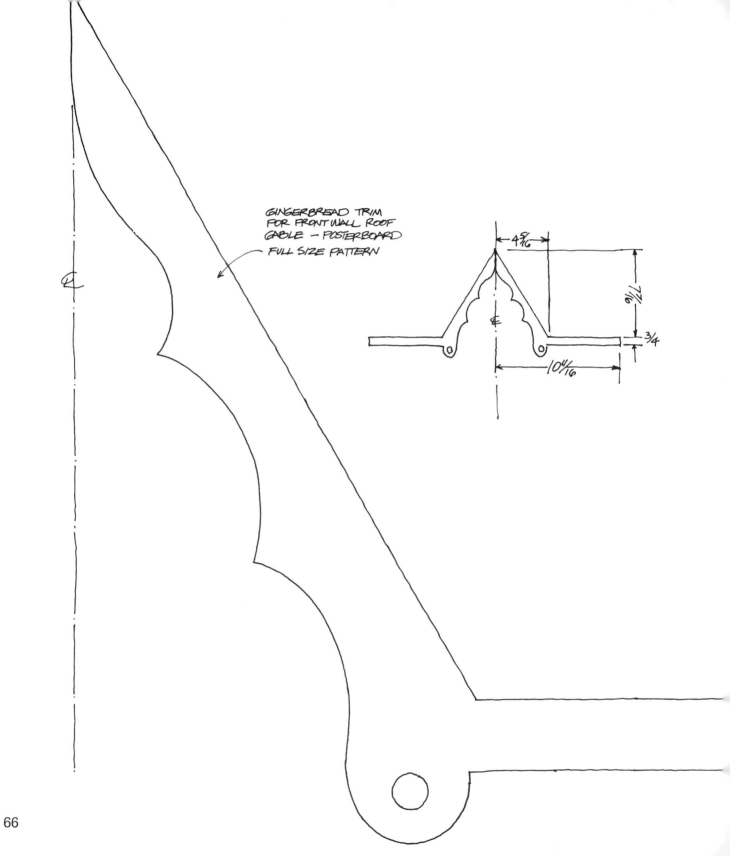

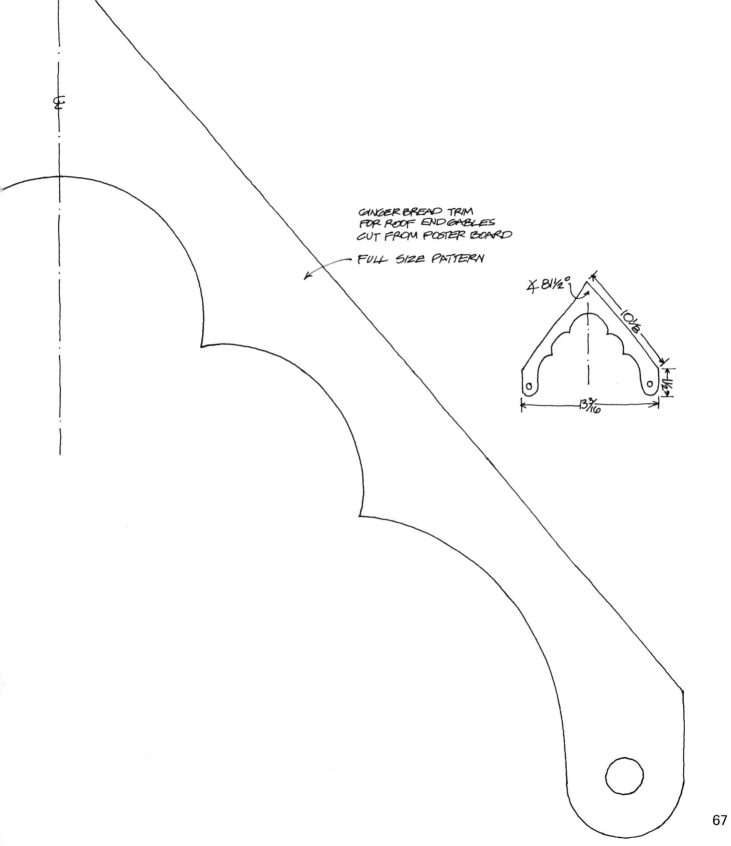

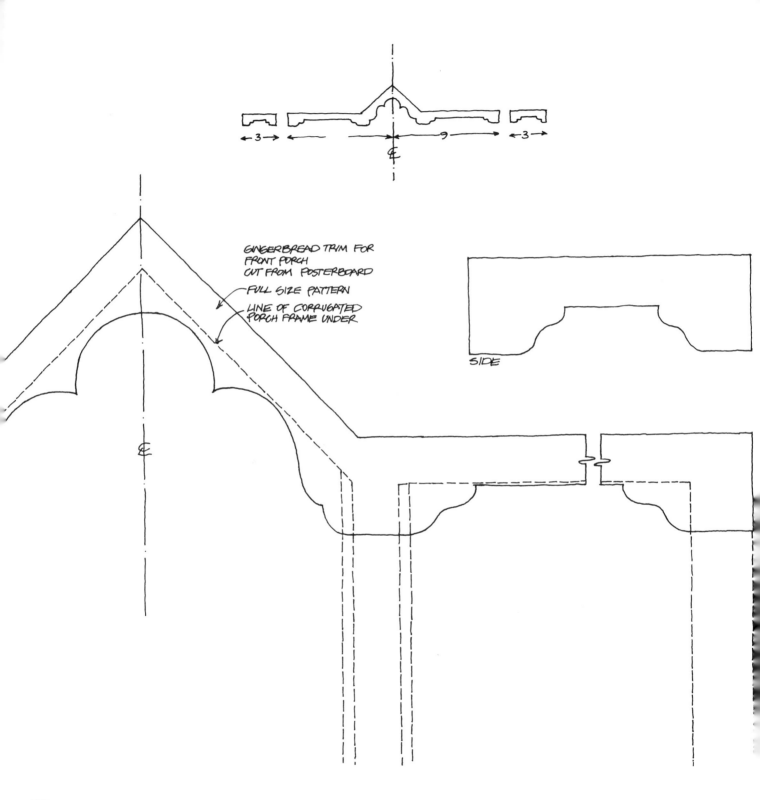

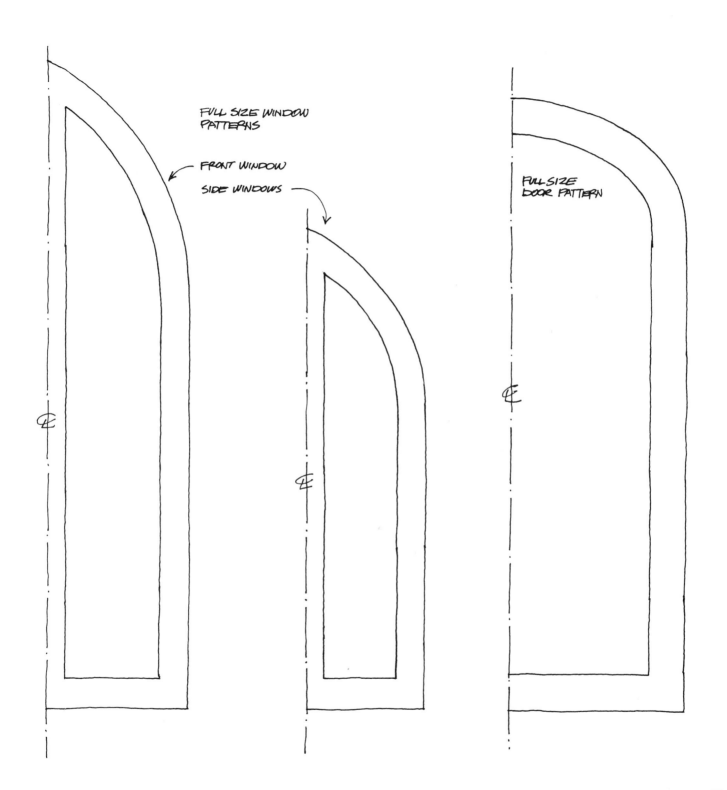

5 Italianate

Around 1845 the Italianate or Italian Villa style, based on Italian country houses, became popular. Italianate is a lyrical style, emphasizing low gabled and hipped roofs with wide eaves supported by ornamental brackets. Square or polygonal towers or cupolas were added to roofs for the views. Round arched windows or arched verandas or porches were popular. Some Italianate designs are asymmetrical with protruding towers and porches forming a complex of shapes. Others are symmetrical, often square in plan. They were constructed out of both wood and masonry in the north, and out of stucco in the warmer southern climates. The Italianate dollhouse is an example of the symmetrical design with a rooftop cupola for looking out across the countryside. These houses were often colored in earth tone shades of ochre or umber.

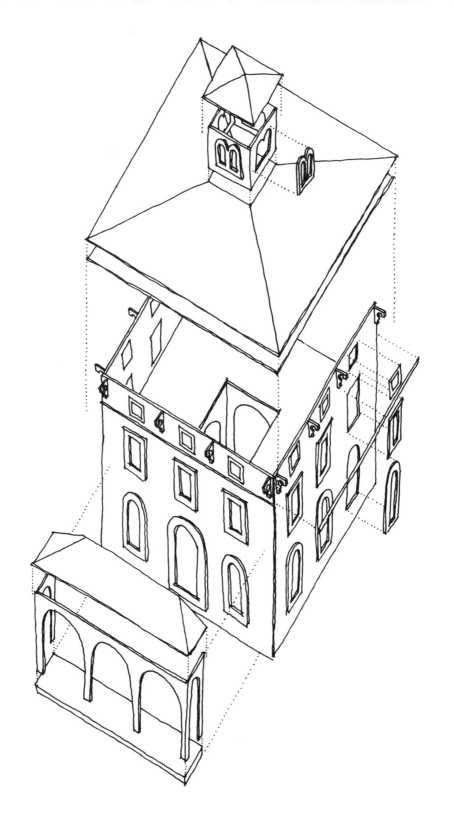

Assembly

1. Glue door and window frames, and horizontal trim strip to walls.

2. Glue 2nd floor support strips to inside of walls.

3. Assemble walls and first floor.

4. Assemble interior pavillion and glue to 2nd floor. Glue into place when dry.

5. Glue second floor ceiling to walls. Make sure it is centered over walls.

6. Assemble roof and glue to ceiling when dry.

7. Add cupola assembly to roof.

8. Fold down flaps on porch floor and glue. Fold porch arches and glue to porch floor.

9. Glue porch floor arches assembly to wall.

10. Add porch roof to wall and arches.

11. Glue brackets to ceiling and walls as shown.

Plans

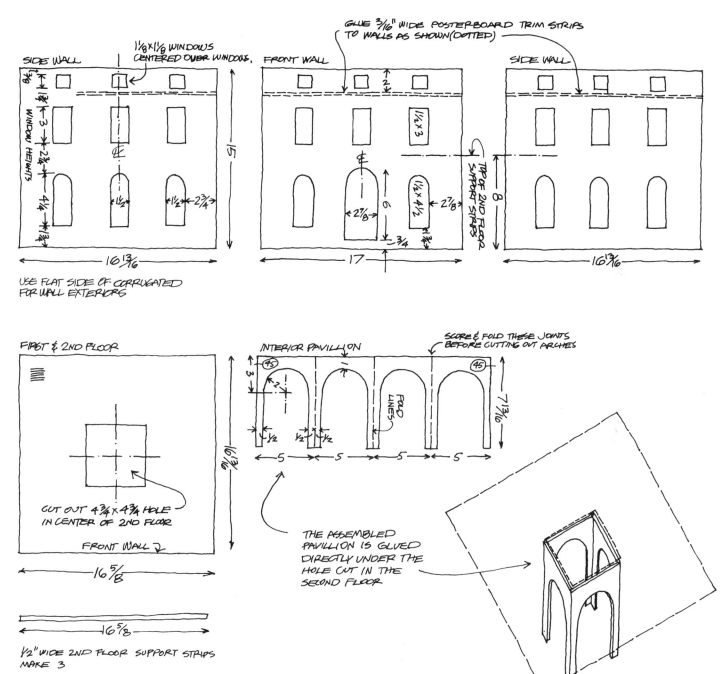

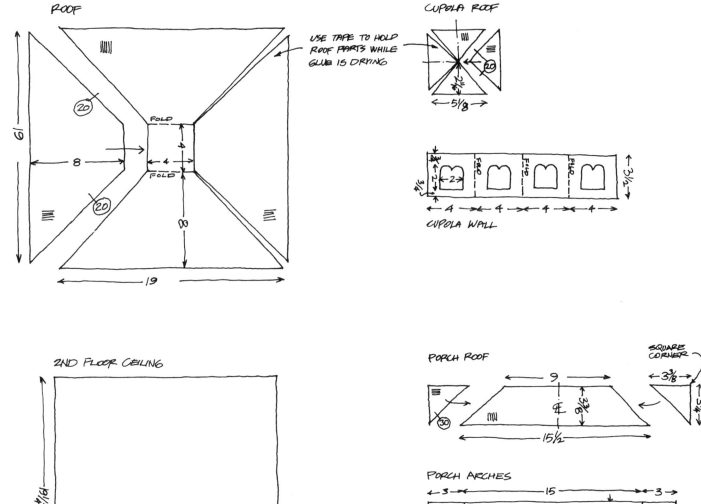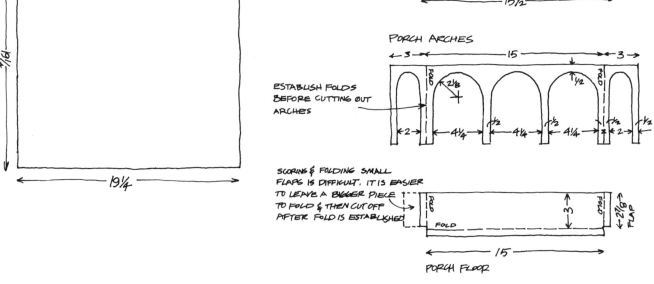

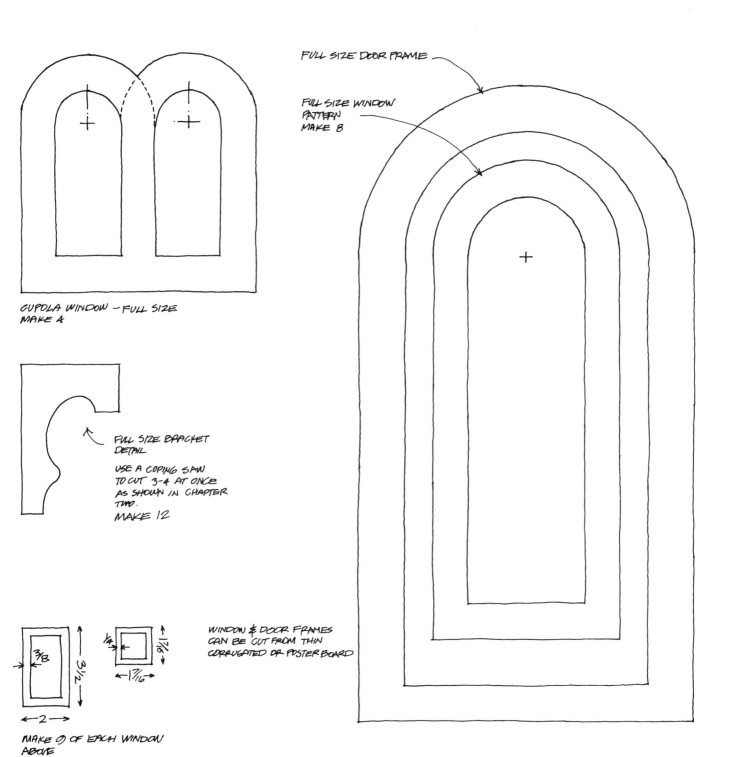

77

Appendix

Corrugated cardboard:

A package of 32" x 40" sheets
$14.50/bundle + shipping.
Item 146101

Order from:

Charrett
212 East 54th Street
New York, New York
10022

Mail order dollhouse
furnishings:

Craft Creative Kits
Dept. 70
North Ave & Rt. 82
Elmhurst, Illinois
60126

Federal Smallwares Corp.
85 5th Ave.
New York, New York
10003